Supplement to *British Book News* : No. 28

E L███████H

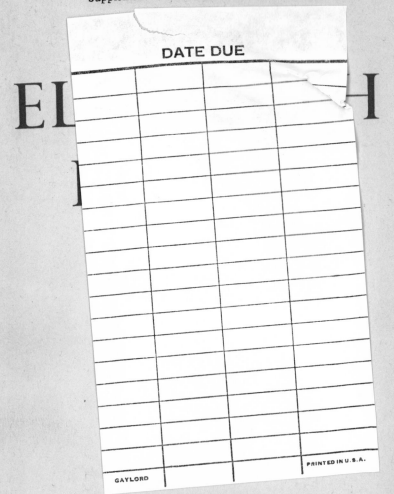

DATE DUE

GAYLORD · PRINTED IN U.S.A.

PUBLISHED FOR
THE BRITISH COUNCIL
and the NATIONAL BOOK LEAGUE
by LONGMANS, GREEN & CO.
LONDON.   NEW YO█

D1213876

Price two shillings net

Mr. Jocelyn Brooke's is a post-war reputation. His first book, *December Spring*, published in 1946, was of poems. This he followed up by an enchanting autobiographical series, *The Military Orchid*, *A Mine of Serpents*, and *The Goose Cathedral*. His other works include *The Image of a Drawn Sword*, *The Scapegoat*, and a book illustrated by Gavin, Muirhead, and Stephen Bone on *The Wild Orchids of Britain*, a subject upon which Mr. Brooke is an authority.

Miss Elizabeth Bowen published her first book, *Encounters*, nearly thirty years ago. It was a collection of stories, and it is as a story-teller and novelist that Mr. Brooke chiefly considers her. Miss Bowen's excursions into other fields have been notable, but it is possibly by her novels that she will best be remembered, for, as Mr. Brooke aptly says, ' Within the acknowledged boundaries of her talent and her temperament, she has created a small and perfect universe which, though wholly her own, can be compared not unfavourably with the world of *Pride and Prejudice*'.

Bibliographical Series
of Supplements to ' British Book News '

★

GENERAL EDITOR
T. O. Beachcroft

ELIZABETH BOWEN

ELIZABETH BOWEN

By JOCELYN BROOKE

PUBLISHED FOR
THE BRITISH COUNCIL
and the NATIONAL BOOK LEAGUE
BY LONGMANS, GREEN & CO., LONDON, NEW YORK, TORONTO

LONGMANS, GREEN & CO. LTD.
6 & 7 Clifford Street, London, W.I
Also at Melbourne and Cape Town

LONGMANS, GREEN & CO. INC.
55 Fifth Avenue, New York, 3

LONGMANS, GREEN & CO.
215 Victoria Street, Toronto, I

ORIENT LONGMANS LTD.
Bombay, Calcutta, Madras

First published in 1952

Printed in Great Britain by Benham and Company Limited
Colchester

ELIZABETH BOWEN

Elizabeth Bowen has often been called a novelist of 'sensibility', a term which, if it means anything at all, is apt too often to imply the exploitation of the writer's own particular temperament at the expense of those other qualities which go to the making of a good novelist. To apply this designation to Miss Bowen is to under-estimate, by implication, the breadth of her talent; and she has herself, as it happens (in a broadcast discussion of her work), specifically denied the impeachment. To her, as a writer, sensibility *in itself* is 'neither here nor there', and it has never been her wish either to 'generate' sensibility for its own sake, or to 'play upon it'. Sensibility is, rather, a kind of medium through which the world can be apprehended more clearly and significantly, just as the features of a landscape will stand out more sharply when seen in a particular kind of light. In other words, Miss Bowen uses her sensibility (which is without question exquisite) as an instrument, merely, for producing the particular effects at which she is aiming in her novels and stories.

What are these 'particular effects' which distinguish her work from that of her fellow-writers? What is it that one chiefly remembers when one has finished a book by Eliza-beth Bowen? She herself has compared her specialized use of sensibility with the light which reveals the beauties of a landscape, and her simile, perhaps, was not quite accidental: for landscape, in the wider sense, is of the first importance in her work, and I think her vivid apprehension of the visible world is, above all else, what makes her writing so memorable. It should not, however, be inferred that Miss Bowen is a writer who indulges in 'flowery' descriptions of nature for their own sake; the reverse is the fact—her descriptive passages are admirably taut and economical, and are without exception closely connected with (and indeed dependent upon) the action of the story. Yet it is, none the less, Miss Bowen's evocations of places—houses, streets,

5

country gardens—which linger in one's memory when, often enough, the story and the characters have been forgotten.

It can be said, at some risk of over-simplification, that novelists are of two kinds : those who are primarily interested in character and situation, and those whose interest lies chiefly in what—for want of a better word—is commonly called 'atmosphere'. Novels by writers of this second category seem to spring from a vision of a 'landscape with figures' rather than from a direct concern with the figures themselves ; it might be termed the visual as opposed to the auditory approach to novel-writing. Compare Miss Bowen's work, for example, with that of Miss Ivy Compton-Burnett[1] : the latter is almost entirely an auditory writer—the visible world is indicated, in her books, in the most perfunctory manner, the story is welded together entirely by means of dialogue, one has a sense of perpetually eavesdropping on her characters. In the case of Miss Bowen, on the other hand, one invariably *sees* her characters before one hears them speak ; they are so much a part of the landscape in which they have their being that one cannot imagine them, even for a moment, as existing in a different setting.

Miss Bowen has admitted that many of her novels and stories had their genesis in the vision of a particular place— a compelling, insistent vision which seemed, as she says (I am quoting again from the broadcast already referred to), to 'draw one into itself'. Only at a much later stage would the characters and their actions emerge, as it were, from the middle-distance into the foreground—and note that I say 'emerge', for there is no question, with Elizabeth Bowen, of grafting a story arbitrarily upon an imagined scene ; the *dramatis personæ*—and the drama itself—are already there, implicit in the landscape of which indeed they form an

[1] See Miss Pamela Hansford Johnson's essay on Miss I. Compton-Burnett in this series (1951).

essential part, though they have yet to be picked out, as it were, by the camera-eye of the novelist's vision.

I have already compared Miss Bowen, in passing, with Miss Compton-Burnett : and it may be worth mentioning that that percipient critic, Mr. Edward Sackville-West, referring to the pictorial quality in Miss Bowen's writing, has remarked that ' she stands in the same relation to Miss Compton-Burnett as Vuillard stands to Braque '. Comparisons between painting and writing are too often apt to misfire, but this one seems to me very much to the point. There is, undoubtedly, a quality in Miss Bowen's writing which suggests the work of the French Impressionists—in particular, one remembers her intense feeling for light ; and it is interesting, in this connexion, to learn that Miss Bowen did, in her early youth, intend to be a painter. Another possible source for this pictorial quality in her work—and especially for her sensitivity to light—is the fact that Miss Bowen has spent much of her life in Ireland, where light is an extremely important factor in the landscape, and can, as Miss Bowen herself has said, ' determine one's mood, one's day, and one's entire sense of the world '. Each of her novels and stories seems, in retrospect, to be lit by its own particular radiance—one remembers, for instance, the ripe, late-summer sunlight of *The Last September*, the bleak, wintry afternoons on the south coast in *The Death of the Heart*, the blanched London moonlight of *Mysterious Kôr*.

This preoccupation with the visible world suggests a further comparison—not with painting, in this case, but with the work of another distinguished woman-novelist of a slightly earlier generation than Miss Bowen's : I mean Virginia Woolf. In Mrs. Woolf's novels one finds the same acute awareness of outside things, the same almost pictorial intensity of vision ; yet Mrs. Woolf tended, I think, to become preoccupied with the thing seen *for its own sake*, whereas, in the case of Miss Bowen, the landscape —however important—is never allowed to swamp the figures who inhabit it. Mrs. Woolf, though she wrote novels, was by temperament a poet ; Miss Bowen, on the other hand, is indisputably a born novelist.

An abnormally acute apprehension of the visible world—this, then, is the outstanding quality which one chiefly remembers about the work of Elizabeth Bowen. But this faculty would not, I think, suffice by itself to make her achievement so memorable ; and though her ' pictorial' view of the social scene is the aspect of her writing most obvious on a first reading, it would be taking an extremely superficial view to say that the visible world is Miss Bowen's main preoccupation as a novelist.

Apart, then, from the visual approach, what other aspects of her work remain most clearly in one's memory ? Plot ? Decidedly no : Miss Bowen's plots are, for the most part, of an extreme simplicity ; indeed, her novels can hardly (with the possible exception of *The Heat of the Day*) be said to have ' plots ' at all. Character ? Again (though less decidedly) no : for Miss Bowen, though an adept at presenting and analysing her characters, is seldom, one feels, passionately concerned with them merely *as* characters ; and, though one remembers many of the people in her books, she cannot be said to have created any ' great ' characters such as those of Dostoievsky, Proust or Dickens.

No : Miss Bowen is not chiefly notable either for plot or for the delineation of character ; but with the consideration of character we do approach nearer to what I feel to be the connecting link between almost all her novels and stories, and the mainspring of her creative achievement. This I would describe as a preoccupation with the *relationship between the individual and his environment*. I have already compared her work to a ' landscape with figures ' ; and if one extends the word ' landscape ' to include the whole social scene, together with its deeper implications, I think the term will stand.

' Deeper implications '—the phrase may seem a cloudy one, but in this context it has, I think, an exact application.

Above all things, Miss Bowen is an exceedingly *civilized* person, both in herself and in her writing—and I am using the word in what I take to be its exact sense. By civilization I mean that complex of habits, tastes, inherited codes of behaviour, etc. which, in a highly organized society, serves as a kind of protective barrier against the barbarous and anarchic elements surviving in that society. Miss Bowen has herself spoken (in the discussion from which I have already quoted) of her fascination with the ' surface ' of life —not so much for its own sake, as for the dangerous sense which it gives of existing upon a thin crust beneath which lurks the bottomless abyss. The crust is, too often, liable to crack—and, says Miss Bowen, ' the more the surface seems to heave or threaten to crack, the more its actual pattern fascinates me '.

As a novelist she is, I think, primarily interested in the *behaviour* of her characters as it is affected by this ' cracking ' or ' heaving ' of the ground upon which they so perilously exist. (Miss Bowen has, in fact, described herself as a novelist of ' behaviour ' as opposed to ' sensibility '.) In this, she recalls Mr. E. M. Forster, in whose novels one is so often similarly aware of the abyss beneath one's feet ; yet there are marked differences between Miss Bowen's treatment of this theme and that employed by Mr. Forster.[1] Miss Bowen is, it seems to me, intent upon preserving the protective ' crust ' intact—fascinated though she is by the ominous fissures which appear in it ; Mr. Forster, on the other hand, recognizes, perhaps more frankly, the existence of the abyss, and is even prepared, on occasion, to dive into its depths and attempt to come to terms with its inhabitants. ' Only connect ' is his watchword—only connect the monk and the beast in man, and you shall be saved. Miss Bowen is perhaps more of a pessimist : she is concerned not so much to ' connect ', as to display the tragic results of the con-nexion which has failed to take place, or which has gone fatally wrong. She is more pessimistic, and also more

[1] See Rex Warner's study of E. M. Forster in this series (1950).

detached ; and it may be added that the particular aspect of the ' abyss ' which fascinates her is, again, different from that which one associates with Mr. Forster. She is, even more than Mr. Forster, concerned with the social behaviour of highly civilized men and women ; she seldom writes about working-class people, and the social group which, for her, represents the intractable and dangerous element in society is not the proletariat (or the near-proletariat—compare the Basts in *Howard's End*) but the pretentious, Philistine middle-class—such families as the Heccombs in *The Death of the Heart* and the Kelways in *The Heat of the Day*.

Mr. Edward Sackville-West, whom I have already quoted in another connexion, has lately proclaimed that the chief persons in a novel—' those whose characters and fate form the apex of the plot or idea—must possess an appreciable education and/or sensibility'. He adds that ' genuine tragedy at a low level of mentality is a contradiction in terms ', and that ' attempts to create it . . . produce an impression of impertinence and moral chaos '. This might be described as the aristocratic as opposed to the democratic view of the Art of Fiction, and it is not a particularly popular view to-day ; but I think that Miss Bowen would agree, in the main, with Mr. Sackville-West's judgement.

Elizabeth Bowen belongs, by her ancestry, to the Anglo-Irish country gentry—the inhabitants of those ' Great Houses ' many of which, in the Southern Ireland of to-day, are mere burnt-out ruins, but whose owners, in the past, have contributed so much to the cultural heritage of these islands. She has inherited Bowen's Court, the family mansion in County Cork, and has spent much of her life there ; to-day she divides her time between England and Eire. Though Anglo-Irish, her family is, in fact, of Welsh origin (the name Bowen derives from ap Owen), so that two separate streams of Celtic blood flow in her veins. Much of her childhood was spent in East Kent (chiefly at Folkestone and Hythe, which appear in several of her novels and

stories) ; later she went to school at Downe House, Wester-
ham (in West Kent), where, unlike most English writers—
male ones, at any rate—she was, on the whole, very happy.
She is married, and has lived in Oxford, London and elsewhere ; she has travelled much, chiefly in France and Italy,
and has several times visited America.

Her first book, *Encounters*—a collection of short stories—
was published in 1923 ; since then, she has been a regular and
prolific writer—her output includes seven novels, several
volumes of stories, a history of her own house and family
(*Bowen's Court*) and a collection of her occasional essays
(*Collected Impressions*), as well as a recently published
historical sketch of the Shelbourne Hotel, Dublin.

It is impossible, in an essay of this length, to discuss all her
work in detail, and I shall concentrate, for the most part,
upon the novels, contenting myself with a comparatively
brief survey of her other work.

Encounters, the early volume of short stories, has lately
been reprinted, and is of considerable retrospective interest. The stories already show an extraordinary maturity,
and a detachment rare in the work of young writers ; they
are for the most part short sketches, each centring about
some (usually) trivial anecdote. What one notices here is
Miss Bowen's sureness of touch : she seems to have been
incapable, even in her earliest days as a writer, of fumbling,
or of ' muffing ' her effects. One notices her interest in the
superficies of life—details of houses, clothes, etc. ; and her
sense of light and atmosphere, though less noticeable than
in her later work, is already much in evidence.

> . . . He saw the family in silhouette against the windows ; the
> windows looked out into a garden closed darkly in by walls.
> There were so many of the family it seemed as though they must
> have multiplied during the night ; their flesh gleamed pinkly
> in the cold northern light and they were always moving.

This passage, from the first paragraph of the first story
(*Breakfast*) in Miss Bowen's first book, is significant : the

man entering the room 'sees the family in silhouette'—a group of people perceived in relation to their surroundings (the windows, the garden beyond, the 'cold northern light'). Already, it is the 'landscape' which makes the primary impact—though this, perhaps, would only be noticeable in the light of Miss Bowen's later work. In most of these short pieces the 'story' is well to the fore—though it is evident enough that the anecdote, in most cases, had its birth in an instant of visual susceptibility : so much, indeed, Miss Bowen admits herself in a new preface to the book, in which she refers to this susceptibility as being 'rendered articulate' by 'places, moments, objects, and times of year'. A notable example is the story *Daffodils*, the lyrical intensity of which seems to have been inspired by the impact of a windy, sunlit March afternoon in a country town.

Ann Lee's, a second collection of stories, followed in 1926. The same qualities are again noticeable, but one detects, also, a subtilizing of Miss Bowen's perceptions, especially in relation to the niceties of social intercourse—a good example is the story which gives its title to the book. *The Hotel*, her first novel, appeared in 1927 ; it describes the life of a group of English people wintering on the Italian riviera, and was largely suggested, I believe, by a winter which Miss Bowen herself spent at Bordighera. The heroine, Sydney, is a highly-intelligent and susceptible young girl whose knowledge of life, largely derived from books, outruns her capacity to cope with the real business of living. (In this respect Sydney is a typical figure of the nineteen-twenties, and might be described as the female counterpart of the young men in the earlier novels of Mr. Aldous Huxley.) *The Hotel* is Miss Bowen's 'lightest' novel, and contains a number of very funny passages ; yet the intention of the book is serious—it might be described as a tragi-comedy— and, in the emotional conflict of the clever yet immature Sydney, one recognizes a hint of that theme which, in her later and more highly-wrought novels, will become one of Miss Bowen's chief preoccupations : I mean the predicament of the 'innocent heart' pitted against the forces of insensibility and misunderstanding, the victim of its own immaturity. It is a theme which, once again, suggests E. M. Forster; and it will recur again and again in the later novels—more especially in *The House in Paris* and *The Death of the Heart*.

In 1929 appeared Miss Bowen's second novel, *The Last September*, and with it she emerges for the first time as a mature and entirely original novelist. Many of her admirers consider it her best novel, and I am almost inclined to agree; Miss Bowen herself has a particular affection for it, and this is understandable, for *The Last September*, more than any of her other books, seems to have been written from the heart. It has, indeed, a quality which can only be called lyrical: the descriptions of the 'Great House' and its demesne linger in the memory with an extraordinary persistence, so that in retrospect the story seems to belong to some far-distant, half-forgotten phase of one's own life.

Lois, the young girl living with her aunt and uncle at the 'Great House' (Miss Bowen calls it Danielstown, but the house is recognizably Bowen's Court), is not so very different from Sydney in *The Hotel*: she is less 'clever', but she, too, typifies the innocent heart at war with an unsympathetic or hostile environment. The action takes place at the time of the 'troubles': the nearby garrison town (Fermoy) is full of British officers, there are dances, tennis-parties and so on; Lois falls in love with a charming young subaltern, Gerald, but her aunt considers him too poor and of insufficiently good family—his people come from Surrey:

... 'All in Surrey?' [asks the aunt.]
'Scattered about.'
'That sounds to me, of course,' remarked Lady Naylor, pulling her gloves off brightly, 'exceedingly restless. ...'

Lady Naylor contrives, by trickery, to estrange the two lovers; then Gerald is killed by the Sinn Feiners. At the end, the house is burnt down—also by the rebels. There are several sub-plots, but this is the main story : once again, the innocent heart is betrayed, and, on this occasion, physical violence plays its part (the death of Gerald)—an uncommon occurrence in Miss Bowen's novels, where the tragedy is, more often, confined to the minds of the characters. (This is perhaps a good moment to point out how seldom Miss Bowen concerns herself with violence in any form ; it may be added, too, that she almost never touches on the subject of physical love or, indeed, upon sexuality at all, except in its most cerebral aspects.)

What one remembers chiefly about *The Last September* is a sense of brooding, nostalgic melancholy : the great doomed house in its rook-haunted demesne, tragedy coming to a climax in the calm, opulent sunlight of an Irish autumn.   Each detail of the scene seems lit by the anguished, hallucinatory radiance of coming disaster : flowers trembling in a vase, a curtain stirred by the wind—these are invested with a pathos, a tragic significance which is echoed, more obviously, in the frivolous social occasions, the dances and flirtations, in which the persons concerned seem largely ignorant yet mysteriously half-expectant of the threatening storm. *The Last September* has been compared with Tchekov, and the comparison is, I think, a just one ; for Elizabeth Bowen, though she is describing a particular situation, contrives, like the Russian playwright, to invest her theme with a universal significance.

The Last September was followed by two novels published in rapid succession—*Friends and Relations* (1931) and *To the North* (1932). *Friends and Relations*, if it lacks the lyrical impulse of *The Last September*, is none the less one of Miss Bowen's most attractive works.   It does not, I think, represent the highwater-mark of her achievement, but in it she seems to develop a new confidence—this, she seems to be saying, is *my* kind of novel, the kind I am best able to write. The accustomed preoccupations recur once more—the theme of betrayal, and the conflict between the rebellious young and their conventional elders ; one could, I think, fairly describe the book as a 'typical' Elizabeth Bowen novel. In her later works, she has broken new ground ; *Friends and Relations* has the charm of an early work combined with a newly acquired professional assurance.

The plot is more complicated than that of the previous novel : put with extreme crudity, its main theme is the shadow cast upon the younger generation by the 'sins of the fathers', though the subject is treated obliquely and, largely, in a vein of comedy. The sinner, in this case, is Lady Elfrida Tilney, a *divorcée* still attached to her ageing lover ; her son, Edward, marries, his children go for a holiday to his sister-in-law's country-house, where his mother is also staying. Edward discovers that his mother's lover is staying there too, and descends upon the house, with a rather feeble vengefulness, to remove the children from the infection of past iniquity. This episode forms, more or less, the climax of the story, and colours, in retrospect, the whole texture of the novel ; I mention it, especially, because it provides an excellent example of that ominous 'cracking' of the social fabric which is such a feature of Miss Bowen's plots. The whole episode is adroitly 'underplayed' ; it is the reverse of dramatic, there is nothing which can be described as a 'scene' ; yet the description of Edward's arrival, subdued though it is, conveys an extraordinary atmosphere of emotional squalor. It is, also, beautifully 'led up to' : Lady Elfrida and the children are shopping in the local country town, it is a hot, thunderous afternoon in summer, the children are plied with ices, in a fly-blown café, by Lady Elfrida's former lover ; they visit the barber's, collect the fish, etc. With a series of brilliant touches, Miss Bowen prepares for her climax : one remembers the deliquescent messiness of the ices, the reek of cheap brilliantine from the little boy's hair—nothing in themselves, but subtly presaging the horror which is lying in wait. Edward arrives : and, from ices and barbers' shops, we are tipped, suddenly, into what E. M. Forster calls 'the world of telegrams and anger'. The smooth, carefully-preserved surface

of life cracks, heaves—for a moment the abyss yawns at
our feet : but only for a moment—for Miss Bowen is
writing of civilized people, and writing of them, moreover,
in terms of (almost) drawing-room comedy.

The comic approach is, in this novel, much in evidence :
the horrible girl Theodora, for instance, who, more than
most of Miss Bowen's characters, is treated with an oblique
but devastating malice :

> ' And of course,' went on Theodora, ' Lady Elfrida does bore
> me.   She's the most tiresome kind of *cathédrale engloutie*, full of
> backwashes and large drowned bells.'
> ' Nonsense ', said Janet kindly, hoping it pleased Theodora
> to be so clever. . . .

One notices also, in *Friends and Relations*, a tendency to-
wards a more complex, highly-wrought style than Miss
Bowen has yet employed.   It is as though—to borrow a
musical term—she had ' thickened ' her score by adding a
whole new range of orchestral effects :

> June afternoon, in Knightsbridge, polished the house-fronts ;
> a crystal twirled in a window ; the young town trees, the cur-
> tains were mildly sensitive to a breeze.   Life in the streets and
> squares ran transparent and ran without a ripple.   A foot on a
> step, a door opening, a taxi stopping engaged the street ; the
> balconies shared a calm social expectancy.   Janet found Lady
> Elfrida's long little drawing-room green, cool, receptive—the
> sun was off it—her hostess quite haggard with the anticipation
> of pleasure.   Lady Elfrida, whose journeys were seldom less
> than transcontinental, ignored the transition from Cheltenham ;
> she did not ask if Janet were tired but, displacing a Siamese cat
> from the sofa beside her, drew Janet down at once to a level of
> intimate talk among the cushions.

In this passage—about 130 words—Miss Bowen contrives, not only to transport Janet from Cheltenham to
London, to describe her meeting with her aunt, and to hit
off the aunt's character with an adroit touch or two (' hag-
gard with the anticipation of pleasure ', etc.), but also to suggest perfectly the atmosphere of a June day in Knightsbridge

—not the weather merely, but the characteristic life and movement of a London street : note, for instance, those balconies with their air of ' calm social expectancy ', and the phrase ' a taxi stopping *engaged* the street '. The word ' engaged ' is exactly right : but how few writers would have hit upon it !

To the North might, like its predecessor, be called a ' typical ' Elizabeth Bowen novel, in that it exploits the territory which its author has made her own, without, to any marked degree, extending it. Cecilia Summers and her sister-in-law, Emmeline, are themselves typically Bowenesque creations ; there are some good satirical portraits—Lady Waters, Gerda Bligh ; but the main interest of the book is undoubtedly Mark Linkwater, the young man with whom Emmeline has a rather half-hearted and unsatisfactory love-affair. Mark is himself, for that matter, both half-hearted and unsatisfactory ; he is a bit of a bounder and (worse still) the sort of bounder who lacks confidence in his own ability to bound—surely the least attractive of his breed. He is interesting, especially, as being Miss Bowen's first full-length portrait of a man (the male characters in the previous novels have all been subsidiary) ; one feels her distaste for this caddish intruder upon the closed, elegant lives of the two women—indeed, one cannot help feeling that she is rather too evidently unsympathetic. Once again the story has a (physically) tragic ending—a motor accident ; but, tragedy apart, *To the North* shows, I think, a growing seriousness in Miss Bowen's treatment of personal relations ; not that humour is lacking—there is the terrible dinner-party, for instance, in Mark's service flat, at which food is ordered by means of a speaking-tube :

> ' But supposing your cook couldn't whistle ? '
> ' I suppose we should have a bell.'
> ' But why don't you have a bell anyhow ? '
> ' I suppose because our cooks can whistle. . . . '
> ' I'm so sorry, Markie,' she said, ' but it sounded as though your cook had got in behind your books—like a cat, you know.'

In its context, this passage is funny, not so much for its own sake, as for its implications ; it is, indeed, more than merely funny—in a subdued way it is rather terrifying, typifying, as it does, the flat, facetious chatter of two lovers who are too frightened of each other and of their situation to talk sensibly.

In *To the North*, as in *Friends and Relations*, one notices again Miss Bowen's growing tendency to ' thicken ' her stylistic effects : the descriptive passages—especially of interiors—become more elaborate, more carefully built-up. It is seldom profitable to try to analyse the influence of other writers upon so highly personal and idiosyncratic a stylist as Elizabeth Bowen : but it may, perhaps, be suggested here that Miss Bowen owes a good deal (but more especially in her latest work) to the example of Henry James.

The next novel, *The House in Paris*, marks a notable stage in Miss Bowen's development, and to some extent represents a break with her previous methods ; before discussing it, therefore, I propose briefly to refer to the collections of short stories which Miss Bowen has published in the intervals between her novels.

Many critics have hailed Elizabeth Bowen as a modern master of the short story, a lineal descendant of Tchekov and Katherine Mansfield ; at one time, indeed—before the appearance of her later novels—it was as a short story writer that she was, perhaps, chiefly celebrated. I think, myself, that her novels are by far her most important achievement ; yet she does, most certainly, deserve all the praise which has been bestowed upon her for her shorter pieces.

I have referred already to the two early collections, *Encounters* and *Ann Lee's* ; since the latter's appearance, Miss Bowen has published four further volumes—*Joining Charles*, *The Cat Jumps*, *Look at all Those Roses*, and *The Demon Lover*. In these one remarks all the qualities which distinguished the earlier volumes—an acute delight in the passing

moment, together with an alert and often malicious obser-
vation of social *nuances*. In the later volumes, however,
one notices also—as one does in the novels—a widening of
perception, implying the need for a more complex tech-
nique ; here again, the ' orchestra ' is being progressively
augmented, and one feels that Miss Bowen is tending more
and more to see things on a number of planes simul-
taneously, so that one is sometimes reminded of those
modern pictures in which several aspects of the same object
are presented in different perspectives on a single canvas. I
think it is this deepening and widening of perception which
has made Miss Bowen turn, increasingly, to the long—or
fairly long—short story ; and it is noteworthy that her
latest volume contains three pieces which might almost be
described as *contes*, rather than short stories in the exact sense
of the term (*Ivy Gripped the Steps, The Inherited Clock, The
Happy Autumn Fields*). *Ivy Gripped the Steps* may be singled
out for special mention : it is an account of a man's return,
in 1944, to the south-coast town which he had known in
childhood. The description of the blitzed, ivy-grown
houses, the desolate streets with their barbed wire and
sandbags, could not be bettered ; and I think, in fact, that
this story is one of Miss Bowen's finest pieces of work.
The *conte*, unfortunately, is an unpopular form in England ;
but it is, I am sure, perfectly suited to a particular facet of
Miss Bowen's talent.

While on the subject of Miss Bowen's short stories, I must
mention one more aspect of her work which is more
apparent in the shorter pieces than in the novels : I mean
her occasional use of the supernatural as a means of gaining
her effects. I say a ' means ', because I do not think Miss
Bowen is very much interested in the supernatural for its
own sake ; she uses it, rather, to heighten or intensify the
horror latent in a situation already conceived in naturalistic
terms. In *The Demon Lover*, for instance, one feels that the
atmosphere which inspired the story—the shut-up, blitzed
house, on an August afternoon—demanded some kind of a

'ghost' as its *raison d'être*. *The Happy Autumn Fields* is a
ghost story of a different kind—a clairvoyant 'flash-back'
to the Victorian past, occasioned by the discovery of a box
of old letters ; the supernatural element is not, in effect,
essential to the story, but serves merely to make it cohere,
and to throw the incidents into relief.

This ' supernatural '—or at least macabre—element in Miss
Bowen's work is hinted at in the next novel to be considered : *The House in Paris*. True, there are no ghosts in
Mme Fisher's *pension*, but the whole book is impregnated
with a brooding, sinister atmosphere which suggests that of
some story by Le Fanu. (Miss Bowen is, by the way, an
admirer of Le Fanu, and has written an interesting intro-
duction to his best-known novel, *Uncle Silas*.) The plot of
The House in Paris might be compared with a figure of
eight : the two loops of the eight are the past and the future,
their point of intersection a day in Mme Fisher's house,
where two children are spending a few hours in the care of
Mme Fisher's daughter. Harriet is *en route*, merely, for
Mentone, where she is to stay with a relation ; Leopold is at
Mme Fisher's for a more important reason : his presence
in the house represents, indeed, a kind of involuted climax
to the lives of the other, grown-up characters, and its implications are tragic. Miss Bowen has often depicted children
as subsidiary characters (cf. *Friends and Relations*), but
Leopold is, in a sense, the hero—or at least the focal point—
of *The House in Paris*. In this novel, more surely and more
movingly than elsewhere, Miss Bowen is dealing with her
favourite theme—the innocent heart as the victim of a
social conspiracy. The fact that Leopold is a child renders
the situation infinitely more poignant ; and his tragic
predicament seems the more excruciating when we realize
that his innocence is, in fact, adulterated by an almost adult
percipience, the precocious slyness of an only child brought
up among grown-ups.

The atmosphere of the stuffy, French *bourgeois* house,

with the evil old woman in her sickroom upstairs, is admirably conveyed ; and Miss Bowen has, I think, achieved an extraordinary *tour de force* in contriving that the long middle section of the book—an extended ' flash-back '—shall not seem incongruous with the opening and closing sections. The life of Leopold's mother, her romantic love-affair, her relationship with Mme Fisher's daughter—all these take us far away from the dark, claustrophobic house and the waiting children ; yet the house remains a focal point in space and time, the whole of the past has, one feels, led up to this gloomy afternoon which, also, holds within it the germ of a future not less tragic than what has gone before. Factually, the book ends on a flat, indeterminate note : but the ripples from that Paris afternoon spread outward into the future as well as into the past ; *The House in Paris* might be described as the prologue to a tragedy yet unwritten.

It is, I think, Miss Bowen's most moving novel, and it has a good claim to be considered her finest. In the two previous works, one felt, despite all her great abilities—her style, her wit, her brilliant analysis of character—that something was lacking ; both books had great moments, one was moved by them—but only intermittently. One could not avoid, in fact, the feeling that an immense and beautiful superstructure had been built upon a foundation insufficiently strong to support it ; and one hoped that in her next novel Miss Bowen would find a theme more fully worthy of her capacities as a writer. *The House in Paris*, to my mind, justifies this hope abundantly : all Miss Bowen's most brilliant qualities are here in evidence—her wit, her descriptive power, above all her sense of the tragic—yet the book is so superbly balanced that one never for a moment feels (as one felt, for example, at moments, in *To the North*), that the ' scaffolding ' is inadequate to support the weight of so much superimposed ornament.

With *The Death of the Heart*, her next novel, Miss Bowen achieved a far wider popularity than she had known before.

One can see why : for in this novel, though she compromises in no way with the high standards which she has set herself, Miss Bowen seems to be writing with an unprecedented liveliness and gusto. In contrast to the somewhat static quality of (for example) *To the North*, *The Death of the Heart* is dynamic, and the narrative moves with an unaccustomed swiftness. The title suggests the theme—once again, the betrayal of innocence ; and I think that *The Death of the Heart* might be regarded as Miss Bowen's final and most perfect statement of the predicament which has for so long engaged her imagination. In this case the victim is Portia, an adolescent girl, living with a not-very-sympathetic family of relations in London. In her loneliness, she turns to the only person who seems to love her—an irresponsible young philanderer called Eddie. Later, she is sent away for a seaside holiday to Seale, on the Kentish coast (' Seale ', by the way, is Hythe, where Miss Bowen spent much of her own childhood) ; the family with whom she stays—the Heccombs—are no more sympathetic than her London relations ; the young man, Eddie, pays her a visit, and Portia falls passionately in love with him. She returns at last to London, the affair with Eddie peters out in misery and misunderstanding, and Portia, on a hysterical impulse, escapes from the house and flings herself upon the protection of a dim friend of the family, a Major Brutt, who has shown an avuncular affection for her in the past. Major Brutt, not surprisingly, betrays her to her family ; and the book closes with the journey across London of the servant who has been despatched to bring her home. Like *The House in Paris*, *The Death of the Heart* is, in a sense, a prologue to tragedy, and its implications are, if anything, more disquieting than those of the earlier novel. Yet the book is, as Miss Bowen herself has pointed out (I quote once again from the broadcast referred to above), not so much a tragedy of adolescence as a tragedy of *atrophy*. It is not, in fact, Portia's predicament, moving though this is, which makes the story so terrifying : it is, rather, the insensibility, the emotional atrophy of the grown-ups who surround her. Portia's function in the novel is (as Miss Bowen adds) to be the one character who is 'awake'; she imparts meaning rather than carries meaning.

Tragic though the book is, however, it will be remembered, by many readers, for its wonderfully sustained passages of satirical comedy. The middle section, describing the Heccomb family with whom Portia stays at Seale-on-Sea, exhibits Miss Bowen's wit at its most excruciating : the Heccombs belong to that social *milieu* which, of all others, Miss Bowen most intensely dislikes, and her gift for satire, restrained and localized in the previous novels, is here given free play. The awful bungalow ('Waikiki') on the seafront, poor, flustered Mrs. Heccomb, bullied by her stepchildren, the children themselves—Miss Bowen writes of the whole household with a kind of fascinated horror : 'Waikiki' is, one feels, her private vision of the abyss, a bleak and windswept inferno on the Kentish coast. The vulgarity of the Heccombs is of that appalling brand which is perhaps only to be found in this country : the borderline snobism of the *déclassé* middle-class, perpetually aping the wrong kind of smartness. They cannot open their mouths without betraying their crass spiritual muddledom, their inability to see the simplest matter in its proper perspective :

'Well, you ought to fly out at Dickie, you ought really. What did he say he'd mend that bell for if he wasn't going to mend it ? No one asked him to say he would mend that bell.'

'It was very good of him, dear. I might remind him at supper.'

'He won't be in for supper. He's got a date. He said.'

'Oh yes, so he did—what am I thinking about ?'

'Don't ask me,' said Daphne kindly. 'However, don't you worry : I'll eat the odd sausage. What is it, by the way ?'

'Egg pie. I thought that would be light.'

'*Light* ?' said Daphne appalled.

'For Portia after the journey. If you want more, dear, we can open the galantine. . . .'

That unopened galantine exhales a horror as potent, in its own way, as the witches' cauldron in *Macbeth*.

The Death of the Heart, if not Miss Bowen's most technically successful novel, is certainly one of her most engaging. *The House in Paris* is, possibly, a finer achievement ; but, speaking for myself, I find *The Death of the Heart* more purely enjoyable, and it is the novel of Miss Bowen's which I find myself most often re-reading.

The Heat of the Day appeared after an interval of eleven years, in 1949. With it, Miss Bowen established her claim to be one of the three or four most important novelists writing in English. This book received higher praise than any other of her works ; it is certainly her most ambitious novel, and if I do not altogether agree with those who say that it is her best, my reason may be largely a personal one. I have spoken before of what I conceive to be the ' typical ' Elizabeth Bowen novel (I was referring, in particular, to *Friends and Relations*), and perhaps the mere fact that *The Heat of the Day* is so atypical makes me inclined to be prejudiced. It is, of course, unfair to Miss Bowen's wide-ranging talent to speak of a ' typical ' novel by her : for her books are far from being ' all of a piece ' in the sense that, for instance, Miss Compton-Burnett's are. Yet it does seem to me that in attempting to grapple with a theme as portentous as that of *The Heat of the Day*, Miss Bowen has been forced to sacrifice some of the qualities which chiefly distinguish her work at its best.

The Heat of the Day is a war-novel ; it is also a love-story. The two should not be mutually exclusive ; yet the chief fault of this novel lies, for me, in a certain dichotomy between these two elements. The plot is melodramatic— it might almost, one feels, have been conceived by Mr. Graham Greene or by Mr. Nigel Balchin. Stella Rodney's lover, Robert Kelway, is suspected of selling information to the enemy ; he is being shadowed by some kind of spy, Harrison, who offers to drop—or at least postpone—the pursuit of Robert if Stella will become his lover. The

situation is curiously improbable, and is not made more
plausible by the vagueness which surrounds the actions of
the two men : one is never sure of the exact nature or scope
of Robert's crime, and Harrison remains a shadowy figure
throughout, haunting Stella like a vengeful but rather in-
effectual ghost. The situation itself is almost as obscure as
that of a story by Kafka : the characters seem to be caught
up in a chain of circumstances whose origin can only—like
the charge against ' K ' in *The Trial*—be guessed at. This is
no doubt intentional ; and Miss Bowen does, one must
admit, produce an effect of terror merely by her significant
omissions : Harrison, for instance, dim and unrealized
though he is, inspires horror by his very vagueness ; one
feels, behind the characterless façade, the menace of sheer
emptiness. In many passages one has the impression that
the characters are inhabiting a kind of limbo, their words
and actions have the deadness of a film in which the sound-
track has suddenly broken down. Especially memorable is
the description of a visit to a café in the blackout : people
fumbling in the dark, lost, and then the sudden emergence
into the neon-lighted, chromium brightness—another of
Miss Bowen's peculiarly horrible infernos. Unforgettable,
too, is the account of Stella's visit to the Kelways, her lover's
family : Holme Dene, the Kelways' house, is a kind of
magnified and more frightful ' Waikiki ', but in this case
Miss Bowen is at once more serious and less merciful in her
treatment of its inmates.

I have spoken already of the dichotomy which exists
between the book's two major themes, and the whole novel
produces, in fact, an effect of disjection, of being composed
of a number of broken fragments, like a jigsaw puzzle in
which the pieces are arbitrarily fitted together, so that the
final picture is distorted. Miss Bowen has, as it happens,
admitted that this—or something like it—was her intention
when writing the book ; the distorted, fragmentary effect
is deliberate, a bold attempt to supply an aesthetic equivalent
to the actual breaking-up of urban life under the stress of

war. (In this respect, *The Heat of the Day* might be compared with *The Waste Land*, in which Mr. Eliot attempted something of the same kind in poetic terms : ' These fragments I have shored against my ruins.')

In her previous novels Miss Bowen has tended (as I have already indicated) steadily to augment her stylistic resources; her prose has become, with each new book, more elaborate, as though the pressure of her material demanded a more complex and comprehensive form for its perfect expression. In *The Death of the Heart*—and especially in the middle, ' Waikiki ' section—there seemed a partial reversion to an earlier, less elaborate treatment, and it was a matter of considerable interest to see whether this would be maintained, or whether Miss Bowen would continue to develop in the direction of an even greater complexity. In fact, she has taken the latter course, and *The Heat of the Day* is written in an extremely highly-wrought style, in which the influence of Henry James, already noticeable in the earlier books, is even more apparent. The prose has an extraordinary tautness and intensity, the syntax seems often to be stretched, like elastic, to near breaking-point ; and here, again, one recognizes Miss Bowen's deliberate intention to fashion a style which shall correspond with the overstrained, strung-up condition of men and women in war-time London. At times, indeed, this tautness gives the effect of some neurotic impediment, a kind of stammer ; and occasionally it may lead to actual obscurity.

Surprisingly, the convoluted style of the merely descriptive passages is extended to the dialogue—surprisingly, because Miss Bowen's dialogue, though always concise and pointed, has, up till now, been almost entirely realistic. In *The Heat of the Day* the characters speak in a manner almost as stylized as those of Miss Compton-Burnett : the two working-class girls, for instance, whose story forms one of the many sub-plots, converse in an extraordinary dialect which bears about as much relation to Cockney as that of Synge's plays to the speech of Irish peasants. This, again, is of course perfectly deliberate : Connie and Louie are, in fact, a fictional experiment, an attempt to present very ordinary people as it were *sub specie œternitatis* ; and if the experiment does not altogether succeed, it is at least a highly interesting one.

Here is Harrison, the counter-spy, speaking to Stella about her lover :

> . . . ' One or two of his haunts would miss his familiar face ; he'd start cooling off one or two of his buddies, and so on. *Not to veer a bit, it might be ever so slightly, would take more nerve than a man humanly has. . . .* '

The last sentence, which I have italicized, is an example of Miss Bowen's deliberate distortion of ordinary speech as a means of heightening its effect ; one cannot imagine a man like Harrison really uttering such a sentence (though almost any of Henry James's characters might) ; yet Miss Bowen is well aware of what she is doing, and if Harrison—like the two girls—strikes one as unreal, one can at least say of him that he is, like Portia in *The Death of the Heart*, a ' required ' character, ' imparting ' meaning rather than ' carrying ' it. Like some mysterious ' official ' in a Kafka novel, he is not so much a character as a disquieting Presence, the vehicle for some deadly and half-apprehended menace.

I have said that, to me, *The Heat of the Day* does not seem the most successful of Miss Bowen's works ; yet its formal and stylistic innovations make it, without a doubt, one of her most interesting, and one looks forward with immense curiosity to her next novel. Personally, I do not think that she can go much further in this particular direction : *The Heat of the Day* is, in any case, a war-novel, and the technical experiments which it embodies are directed to a particular end. The earlier books, on the other hand, dealt with a world which has, for all practical (and literary) purposes, ceased to exist : the crust of civilized life has been cracked in too many places, the abyss beneath our feet can no longer be ignored. *The Last September*, consciously elegiac, was also, in a sense, prophetic : for the way of life described in (say) *Friends and Relations* or *The Death of the Heart* has become for us, to-day, as remote (and as potently nostalgic) as the world of Danielstown. What will be Miss Bowen's approach, as a novelist, to the squalid, standardized and unhopeful world in which we are now living ?

To assess the achievement of any imaginative writer is, at the best of times, a thankless task for the critic ; for writers have an inconvenient habit of evading the neat little categories which the critic has prepared, like so many traps, to receive them. When the writer under discussion is not only still living, but in the prime of life and liable, for all one knows, to double or treble his output up to date, the critic's task becomes more difficult still. In the case of Miss Bowen, however, the present moment seems not unfavourable for a retrospective survey of her work, for, though she may well write more and even better novels, it seems unlikely (as I have tried to indicate when discussing *The Heat of the Day*) that she will continue to write in quite the same manner. Her published works can, therefore, be viewed as a whole, without too much risk of unfairness.

I began this essay by remarking that Miss Bowen was widely regarded as a novelist of ' sensibility '. She has, herself, denied the charge, but however much she (and I) may dislike the word, one cannot avoid the conclusion that her *use* of sensibility, as a medium for apprehending the world about her, is a very important factor in her work. With it is linked her extreme susceptibility to and delight in the visible world : no novelist before her has been better able to convey the appearance and atmosphere of (say) a London drawing-room on an August afternoon, or of a sunny winter's morning in a seaside town. I have compared this visionary faculty with that of the great Impressionist painters, and I think it is this pictorial quality in her work which, more than anything else, distinguishes it from that of other novelists. The word ' impressionism ' is apt to suggest a certain vagueness ; but the Impressionists themselves were far from being vague, and in fact based their methods of work upon strictly scientific principles. The same might be said of Elizabeth Bowen : for she is, above all, a highly conscious and deliberate artist ; nothing in her work is left to chance, none of her effects is unpremeditated. She remains always (or very nearly always) aloof, detached from her characters—she has been blamed, indeed, for being, at times, almost too detached. Yet when I say that she is a highly *conscious* writer, I do not mean to imply that her approach to her material is in any sense academic or ' cold-blooded '—far from it. What I am trying to convey is that, like a painter, she is constantly standing back and *looking* at her work : however strong the impulse to ' dash off ' a passage, she will never allow the impulse to take complete control. In her *Notes on Writing a Novel* (included in her *Collected Impressions*) she has explained in great detail her methods of work ; and from these notes it might be inferred (if one had not read her novels) that her extreme detachment would have an inhibiting effect upon the free play of her imagination. In fact, there is no such inhibition : one is aware, as one reads her books, that she is acutely conscious of what she is doing, but one never has the feeling—as one has with some of our more self-conscious contemporary writers—that one is assisting at some complex and difficult experiment in a laboratory. With Miss Bowen one feels that the laboratory work has been completed beforehand and in private ; and the finished product, though plainly marked with the maker's name, has the disarming (though deceptive) air of an improvisation.

Miss Bowen then, it must be admitted, is, in a qualified sense, a novelist of ' sensibility ' ; she is also a highly-conscious artist ; nor must one forget, in summing up her achievement, a fact which, up till now, I have purposely not emphasized—the fact, I mean, that she is a woman. It might not be important ; but in Miss Bowen's case I think it is, for she has from the first, I should guess, taken into account both the limitations and the specific advantages of her femininity. Many women novelists have too boldly assumed that, in matters of art, their sex ceases to be important, and have, in consequence, ignored the limitations which (whether they like it or not) are implied by the mere fact of being female. Miss Bowen has never fallen into this error, and has, I think, deliberately confined herself, in her writing, to the themes which she feels to be safely within her range as a woman novelist. In *The Heat of the Day* one does, perhaps, detect a certain impatience with this self-imposed restriction ; but even here Miss Bowen has not attempted, to any considerable degree, to overstep the bounds which she has set herself. Nobody, it is true, can predict the manner in which a novelist will develop ; but one can be fairly certain that Miss Bowen will not be tempted to write (for instance) a novel about coal-miners or the habits of prize-fighters.

I believe, myself, that at the present stage of her development she is able best to exploit her talent in the form of the long-short story ; her best work is, after all (and among her best I include her novels), conceived on a relatively small scale : her speciality is the minor yet significant *incident*, whether humorous or tragic, not the major *event*. If one uses the term ' great novelist ', one cannot quite avoid the implication of size and weight, Tolstoy and Proust hover in the background, and one finds oneself, if one is not careful, envisaging a novel such as *The Last September* against the background of, say, *War and Peace*. Considered in such terms, Miss Bowen cannot, of course, be regarded as a ' great ' novelist—but nor, for that matter, can Jane Austen ; and it is, I think, Miss Austen, among distinguished novelists of the past, with whom Miss Bowen has most in common. Like Miss Austen she knows her own limitations ; but, within the acknowledged boundaries of her talent and her temperament, she has created a small and perfect universe which, though wholly her own, can be compared not unfavourably with the world of *Pride and Prejudice*.

ELIZABETH BOWEN

A
Select Bibliography

Collected Editions :

SELECTED STORIES, edited by R. Moore (1946).
COLLECTED IMPRESSIONS (1950). *Essays.*
COLLECTED EDITION, Cape (1948 continuing).

Separate Works :

ENCOUNTERS (1923). *Stories.*
ANN LEE'S (1926). *Stories.*
THE HOTEL (1927). *Novel.*
THE LAST SEPTEMBER (1929). *Novel.*
JOINING CHARLES (1929). *Stories.*
FRIENDS AND RELATIONS (1931). *Novel.*
TO THE NORTH (1932). *Novel.*
THE CAT JUMPS (1934). *Stories.*
THE HOUSE IN PARIS (1935). *Novel.*
THE DEATH OF THE HEART (1938). *Novel.*
LOOK AT ALL THOSE ROSES (1941). *Stories.*
SEVEN WINTERS, Dublin (1942). *Autobiography.* Published in London, 1943.
BOWEN'S COURT (1942). *History.*
ENGLISH NOVELISTS (1942). *Criticism.*
THE DEMON LOVER (1945). *Stories.*
ANTHONY TROLLOPE : A NEW JUDGMENT (1946). *Play.*
THE HEAT OF THE DAY (1949). *Novel.*
THE SHELBOURNE (1951). *History.*

Note : Elizabeth Bowen has edited *The Faber Book of Modern Stories* (1937) and has written introductions to *Uncle Silas* by J. S. Le Fanu (1947), and to *Pride and Prejudice* by Jane Austen (1948).

Some Critical Studies :

THE NOVEL SINCE 1939, by Henry Reed (1946).

INCLINATIONS, by E. Sackville-West (1949).

THE NOVEL, 1945–50, by P. H. Newby (1951).

Messrs. Cape publish the following volumes at 7*s.* 6*d.* net each in a uniform edition : *The Last September, The Death of the Heart, The House in Paris, The Cat Jumps, To the North,* and *The Hotel.* The same firm publish at 8*s.* 6*d.* net *Friends and Relations, Look at all Those Roses, Joining Charles,* and *The Demon Lover.* Messrs. Harrap publish *The Shelbourne* at 15*s.* net.

¶ THE Supplements to *British Book News*, which are usually published on the last Monday in each month, may be subscribed for through booksellers on a yearly or half-yearly basis. A year's issues cost £1 post free ; six months' cost 11s. post free. Prospectuses are available ; and particulars of Supplements already published will be found overleaf. Inquiries should be addressed to booksellers, or in case of difficulty direct to the Publishers, LONGMANS, GREEN & CO., 6 & 7 Clifford Street, London, W.1.

BRITISH BOOK NEWS

A monthly bibliographical journal designed to acquaint the reader with the best British books on all subjects, including those published in the Commonwealth and Empire. It contains bibliographies of specific subjects, and articles of general interest to the bookman. Its most important feature is the Book List, compiled by a number of specialists, which occupies the major part of each issue and provides a critical selection of the most important new books and reprints of all kinds, annotated, classified, and indexed.

2s. per copy (United Kingdom)

1s. per copy (Overseas)

Annual subscription 10s. (Overseas)

Bound volumes, fully indexed, are available as follows through LONGMANS, GREEN & CO., 6 & 7 Clifford Street, London, W.1 : for 1943 and 1944, 6s. net each ; for 1945, 7s. 6d. net ; for 1946, 12s. 6d. net ; for 1947, 15s. net ; for 1948 and 1949, 15s. net each ; 1950 is in preparation 15s. net.

¶ *British Book News* is published for the British Council by the National Book League. Address, BRITISH BOOK NEWS, 65 Davies Street, London, W.1.

Supplements to
BRITISH BOOK NEWS
★

BERNARD SHAW	A. C. Ward
JOSEPH CONRAD	Oliver Warner
	…pher Hollis
	…llis Bentley
	…chael Swan
	…d Blunden
	…ex Warner
	…Bradbrook
	…winnerton
	…rbert Read
	…een Raine
	…Dorward
	…e Brander
	…ce Cooper
	…r Fulford
	…d Warner
	…H. Plumb
	…Darlington
	…y Dobrée
	…d Johnson
	…ott-James
	…n Brophy
	…Gascoyne
	…G. Strong
	…Lehmann
	…Tillyard
	…B. Stern
	…say ;

PUBLISHED FOR
THE BRITISH COUNCIL
and the NATIONAL BOOK LEAGUE
by LONGMANS, GREEN & CO.
LONDON. NEW YORK. TORONTO.

2*s.* net